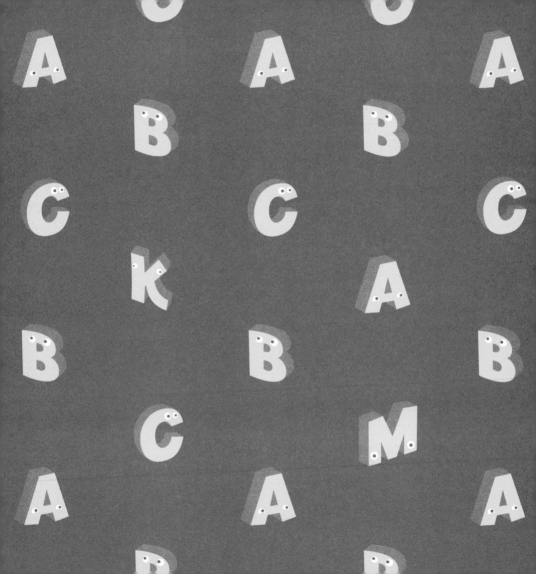

K is for KNIFEBALL

an alphabet of TERRIBLE advice

by Avery Monsen and Jory John

CHRONICLE BOOKS

SAN FRANCISCO

Library of Congress Cataloging-in-Publication Data

Monsen, Avery.
K is for knifeball : an alphabet of terrible advice / by Avery Monsen and Jory John.
p. cm.
ISBN 978-1-4521-0331-0
1. American wit and humor. 2. Alphabet books. I. John, Jory. II. Title.

PN6231.A45M66 2012
818'.602—dc23

2012005872

Manufactured in China

Designed by Avery Monsen

Background textures for some images by Hillary Luetkemeyer (hibbary.deviantart.com).

10 9 8 7 6 5 4 3

Chronicle Books LLC
680 Second Street
San Francisco, California 94107
www.chroniclebooks.com

To our parents. We're so sorry.

Now listen up, youngster.
(Yes, you with the lice.)
We wrote you this book.
It's chock full of advice.
But before you proceed,
little dudette or dude,
sign your name on the line
so that we don't get sued.
By signing this waiver,
you hereby declare
that you won't get a lawyer.
You promise.
You swear.

A is for apple.
Eat one every day.
And then wash it down
with your mom's Cabernet.

B is for blender.
Your daddy won't mind
if you drop in his Rolex
and set it to "GRIND."

C is for cop
with a big, shiny gun.
Sneak up and tickle him!
That'll be fun!

D is for drifter
who's out on your lawn.
Bring him inside when
your parents are gone.

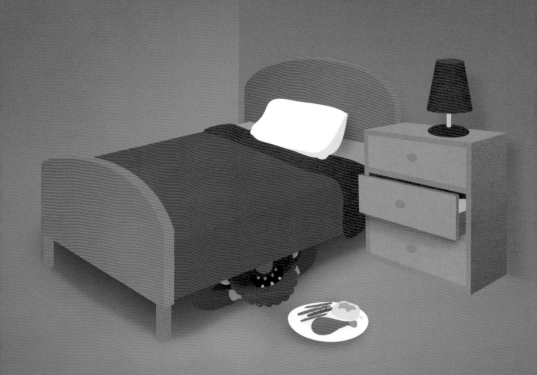

D's also for dinner.
There's plenty to eat.
He's under your bed;
sneak your drifter some meat.

E stands for eat
just as much as you can.
Eat ice cream and waffles
and turkey and ham.

Eat pickles and tuna fish,
milkshakes and figs!
Eat pencils and stencils and
thumbtacks and twigs!

Eat baskets of beard hair!
Eat mountains of mud!
And wash it all down
with a bucket of blood!

F is for fire,
made with logs and a lighter.
Throw Daddy's wallet in.
It'll burn brighter!

Now Daddy is shouting
like you've never heard.
And he keeps repeating
a different F word.

G is for Grandma.
Remind her that she'll be dead soon.

H: Hide and seek!
It's a great game to play.
Quick! Climb in here!
They'll be searching all day.

I's for identity:
easily stolen.
Just take some guy's credit card.
BOOM! Now you're Nolan.

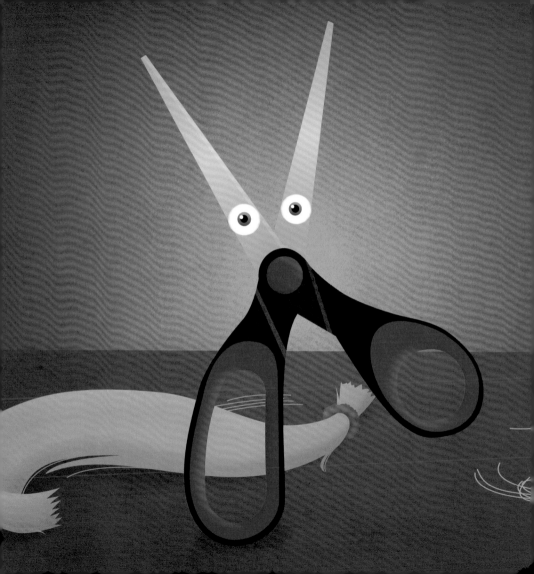

J is for justice.
Make sure things are fair.
If somebody wrongs you,
just cut off their hair.

K is for knifeball.

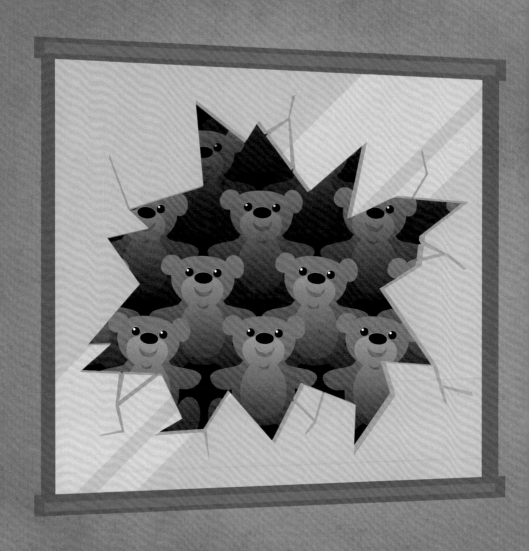

L is for looting.
It's time for a spree.
Throw a rock through a window!
The toys are all free!

M is for marker,
your #1 tool
for writing your name
on the walls of your school.

PERMANENT

N is for nozzle,
the end of the hose.
Water the carpet and
watch how it grows!

O is for open things
up with your teeth.
If your molars fall out,
more will grow underneath!

P is for push
when you're waiting in line.
Do you want to move forward?
Just aim for the spine.

Q is for quit
at the first sign of struggle.
As long as you ... um ...
Q is for ... whatever.

[We'll figure out a drawing for this later.]

R's for raccoon
that you meet on the street.
There's foam on his mouth because
he's been drinking root beer floats
and he probably wants to share
them with you!

R has nothing to do with rabies.

S stands for sun
that shines bright every day.
How long can you stare at it?
Don't look away!

T's for tattoo.
It's never too early
to ink up your body and
start acting surly.

T's also for tombstone.
But who is it for?
Your grandmother, silly!
She was found on the floor.

U is for undies.
They cover your stuff.
Wash them or don't.
Mostly clean's clean enough.

D is for drifter.
He's still in your house.
He's wearing your shoes and
your mom's nicest blouse.

V is for veggies
your parents prepare.
They're guaranteed poison.
All eaters beware.

W? Washer,
for T-shirts and jeans.
It's also for kitty!
He needs a good clean.

Y IS FOR YELL,
AS IN SCREAM EVERY WORD. SHRIEKING'S THE EASIEST WAY TO BE HEARD.

And **Z**s are the sounds that you make when you snore. Rest up, little buddy, tomorrow there's more!

We hope you've learned
something you'll never forget
from our little book
and our alphabet.
Be patient, young reader,
and soon you will see:
Our teachings can make you
the best you can be!

With that, we are finished.
Our gospel is spread.
By the time that you read this,
we've probably fled. To Cambodia.

They don't have an extradition
treaty with the U.S.

ACKNOWLEDGMENTS

First and foremost, thank you, dear reader, for trying everything mentioned in this book. Nice going and sorry about all your shattered bones.

Thanks to our families: Deb, Gail, Bill, and Risa. We don't like a lot of people, but we like you. We'll try to call more.

Thanks to our friends, for sticking by us even though we keep demanding that you "like" our stuff on Facebook. We know it's awful. We're sorry.

Thanks to Steven Malk, who opened up his heart, his home, and his elliptical machine to a couple knuckleheads with a dream.

A huge thanks to everyone at Chronicle Books, especially Steve, Courtney, Emily, Emilie, Erin, April, Albee, and Alison. We're so happy to be a part of the Chronicle family. Is there any chance you can get us health insurance?

ABOUT THE AUTHORS

Avery Monsen and Jory John are the authors of *All My Friends Are Dead*, *Pirate's Log: A Handbook for Aspiring Swashbucklers*, *I Feel Relatively Neutral About New York*, and *All My Friends Are Still Dead*. They also created *Open Letters*, a comic panel which appears in newspapers across the country.

Individually, Jory also writes for newspapers and Avery performs at the Upright Citizens Brigade Theatre in New York.

In their spare time, they make T-shirts at *bigstonehead.net*.

Follow them on Twitter: @averymonsen and @joryjohn.

You can send them letters, c/o the Kingdom of Cambodia.

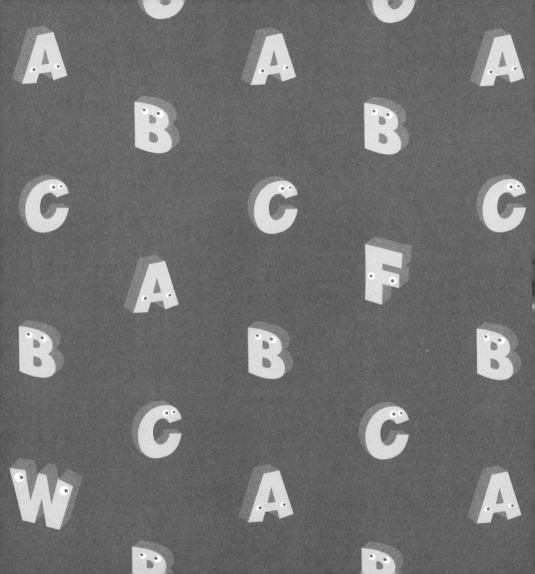

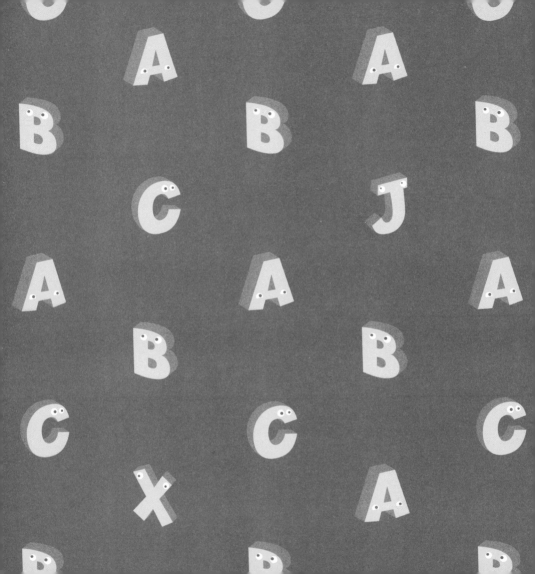